We Can Go

Level 2 – Red

Helpful Hints for Reading at Home

The graphemes (written letters) and phonemes (units of sound) used throughout this series are aligned with Letters and Sounds. This offers a consistent approach to learning whether reading at home or in the classroom.

HERE IS A LIST OF PHONEMES FOR THIS PHASE OF LEARNING. AN EXAMPLE OF THE PRONUNCIATION CAN BE FOUND IN BRACKETS.

Phase 2			
s (sat)	a (cat)	t (tap)	p (tap)
i (pin)	n (net)	m (man)	d (dog)
g (go)	o (sock)	c (cat)	k (kin)
ck (sack)	e (elf)	u (up)	r (rabbit)
h (hut)	b (ball)	f (fish)	ff (off)
l (lip)	ll (ball)	ss (hiss)	

Phase 3 Set 6			
j (jam)	v (van)	w (win)	x (mix)

Phase 3 Set 7			
y (yellow)	z (zoo)	zz (buzz)	qu (quick)

HERE ARE SOME WORDS WHICH YOUR CHILD MAY FIND TRICKY.

Phase 3 Tricky Words			
he	you	she	they
we	all	me	are
be	my	was	her

TOP TIPS FOR HELPING YOUR CHILD TO READ:

- Allow children time to break down unfamiliar words into units of sound and then encourage children to string these sounds together to create the word.

- Encourage your child to point out any focus phonics when they are used.

- Read through the book more than once to grow confidence.

- Ask simple questions about the text to assess understanding.

- Encourage children to use illustrations as prompts.

PHASE 3 /w/

This book focuses on the phoneme /w/ and is a red level 2 book band.

Can you say this sound and draw it with your finger?

We can go in it.

I will go up and up.

I can go on the bus.

We will sit on the bus.

I can go in the wet mud.

I can bob.

I am up the hill. I win!

We can go back.

©2022 **BookLife Publishing Ltd.**
King's Lynn, Norfolk PE30 4LS

ISBN 978-1-80155-094-9

All rights reserved. Printed in Poland.
A catalogue record for this book is available from the British Library.

We Can Go
Written by Rod Barkman
Designed by Gareth Liddington

An Introduction to BookLife Readers...

Our Readers have been specifically created in line with the London Institute of Education's approach to book banding and are phonetically decodable and ordered to support each phase of the Letters and Sounds document.

Each book has been created to provide the best possible reading and learning experience. Our aim is to share our love of books with children, providing both emerging readers and prolific page-turners with beautiful books that are guaranteed to provoke interest and learning, regardless of ability.

BOOK BAND GRADED using the Institute of Education's approach to levelling.

PHONETICALLY DECODABLE supporting each phase of Letters and Sounds.

EXERCISES AND QUESTIONS to offer reinforcement and to ascertain comprehension.

CLEAR DESIGN to inspire and provoke engagement, providing the reader with clear visual representations of each non-fiction topic.

AUTHOR INSIGHT:
ROD BARKMAN

Rod Barkman is one of BookLife Publishing's most integral members. Known to other staff as Reliant Rod, he is always trying to bring his work to a new level. Rod has written multiple books for BookLife Publishing, of which he is extremely proud. Rod is a keen traveller, voracious reader and animal lover.

PHASE 3 /w/

This book focuses on the phoneme /w/ and is a red level 2 book band.

Image Credits Images are courtesy of Shutterstock.com. With thanks to Getty Images, Thinkstock Photo and iStockphoto. Cover – BlueberryPie, Kichigin, Petr Student, Pressmaster, gokturk. p4–5 – Miljan Zivkovic, AShvets. p6–7 – Monkey Business Images, Olesia Bilkei. p8–9 – Zsolt Biczo, Liudmila P. Sundikova. p10–11 – Another77, fizkes.

BookLife Non-Fiction Readers

EXPLORE A WORLD OF NON-FICTION WITH OUR DECODABLE READER RANGE

 9781839278938

 9781839278921

 9781839278945

 9781839278952

 9781839278976

 9781839278969

 9781839278990

 9781839278983

 9781839279010

 9781839279003

 9781839279027

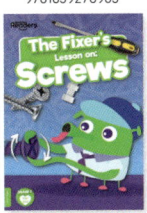 9781839279034

 9781839279058

 9781839279041

MORE COMING SOON

BookLife Readers

The BookLife Readers begin with the very basics of **phonetically decodable reading**. Starting with the earliest step of **CVC** words – words comprising a consonant, a vowel and a consonant – and building on this combination slowly, the reader follows a prescribed format taken directly from the recognised **Letters and Sounds** educational document.

By aligning our books with Letters and Sounds, we offer our readers a consistent approach to learning, whether at home or in the classroom. The illustrations guide the reader, helping to deliver reading progression through the scheme in a **colourful** and **exciting** way. As a reader moves through the book band levels, the page numbers, level of repetition and sentence structure complexity all advance at a rate which **encourages development** without halting enjoyment.

To find out more about this exciting new reading scheme, visit **www.booklife.co.uk**